# I'm Proud of Who I Am
## I Hope You Are Too

### By: B. Woster

BOOK FIVE

©2021 Barbara Woster
ALL RIGHTS RESERVED
Hardcover ISBN: 9781736739471
Paperback: 9781736739488
Ebook ISBN: 9781736739495

Dedication:

To my family without whose love and support this book would never have been written.

The characters in these books are fictitious. Any similarity to real persons, living or dead, is coincidental and not intended by the author. While the characters are fictitious, the author did use real people as inspiration for her characters' future aspirations. Examples: reporter, poet, occupational therapist.

The places are genuine, as are the facts associated. All are presented with the utmost humility and respect to individuals residing in those countries.

No part of this book may be reproduced, stored in a retrieval system, or transmitted, without written permission from the publisher, in any form: electronic, mechanical, photocopying, recording.

## List of countries featured in BOOK FIVE

Aruba
Cape Verde
El Salvador
Guadeloupe
Japan
Kentucky_USA
Liechtenstein
Macedonia
Micronesia/Polynesia/Melanesia
Portugal
Serbia
Sierra Leone
Spain
Swaziland
Tajikistan
Tuvalu
Venezuela
Western Sahara
Wyoming_USA

## Prologue

Have you even once on a clear evening stepped outside or peered from your bedroom window to look up into the night sky, to stare at the stars? I have on many a night. What do I see? I see twinkling lights. You may not see that. You may see the potential of other worlds, or balls of fire, or...nothing wonderous at all. In that we are all very dissimilar. But the fact that we all look at the stars, shows how very much alike we really are.

That is the purpose of this book, to demonstrate that even though we all live in different parts of the world, speak a different language, serve a different god, have different customs, have skin colors that vary in shades from alabaster to deepest brown, and hair color in every hue imaginable...we are more alike than we are different.

We all breathe, eat, drink, live, bleed, and die...and we all have our dreams to which we aspire. We all reach for those stars.

# My Name is Keven

I am from Aruba in the Caribbean Sea. It's a tiny island compared to some of our neighbors, but here's a good way to find it if you look on a map. Find the island of Haiti/Dominican Republic on the north side of the sea. Now run your finger down to the south side. Stop just before you get to Venezuela, South America. That's where Aruba is.

Aruba may be small, but we have a few things that we are mighty proud of. For instance, have you ever heard of pictographs? The inhabitants of Aruba, thousands of years ago, were called Caiquetio shamans. In our caves and on our rock formations, there are many prehistoric drawings that have survived for millennia. Over 300 of them. That's a lot for such a tiny island. You can find them easily if you like rock climbing or spelunking. Spelunking is when you climb around in caves. To find our pictographs, you would want to spelunk through Fontein and Guadirikiri caves[1] because that's where most are found.

Another thing that is unique about Aruba is that it's home to a burrowing owl that you can only find on our island. They're one of those special birds that aren't primarily nocturnal like most owls are, so you can see them, even in the daytime, especially if you're hiking around where cactus is. If you prefer the water to a dry desert area...well, you'll be in good company because we Arubans love the water. I wonder why. Couldn't be because we're surrounded by it. Even though we love swimming, we also love sports that take place on the water. Is there a water sport you're fond of? I love to windsurf. That's like skateboarding on water, but with a sail. I plan to be a professional windsurfer one day. Maybe I will become good enough to beat my hero's championship records. I don't know though; she's won quite a few titles. Look her up sometime. Her name is Sarah-Quita Offringa. She makes us Arubans proud, as I hope to one day.

My name is Keven, and I am proud of who I am. I hope you are too.

---

[1] https://matadornetwork.com/notebook/16-facts-aruba-will-surprise/

# My Name is Elica

I am 15 years old and I live on Cape Verde. Another name for our island chain is Cabo Verde. I call it a chain because there are ten volcanic islands that make up Cape Verde, which, by the way, is in the Atlantic Ocean. If I could share something of interest with you about Cape Verde, it would be the thing I find most fascinating: Loggerhead turtles.

Okay, I do like turtles, but that's not what's fascinating. Did you know that a lot of turtle species are becoming endangered? Well, on one of our islands—Boa Vista—the Loggerhead can come and nest safely. In fact, it is third largest nesting grounds for the Loggerhead Turtles in the world and they have been coming to Boa Vista for thousands of years[2]. Turtles are not the only animals that come to Cape Verde to breed, so do Humpback whales, so if you love whales, Cape Verde is the place to come to see lots of them—during mating season, at least.

As much as I love turtles, and whales, I don't want to work with them when I grow up. What I want to do is to continue to excel in math and science, so that I can one day work as an Aerospace Engineer. What does an Aerospace Engineer do? They are the people who design aircraft and anything else designated for space, whether it's space travel or just to be out in space, like satellites.

My name is Elica, and I am proud of who I am. I hope you are too.

---

[2] https://www.capeverde.co.uk/blog/10-interesting-facts-about-cape-verde

# I am Reny

I live in El Salvador and my passion is computers; especially learning to write code. My specialty, right now, is HTML code, but I am also studying JavaScript and Visual Basic. I wrote the code for my own website and have written code for family and friend's websites too. At 15 years old, I am not able to work doing code for businesses, but if they knew how good I was at it now, they'd hire me. Imagine how good I'll be with a few more years of practice. I look forward to doing what I love.

Speaking of what I love, I love my country, but there is something about it that scares some people. Do you live in a place with volcanoes? Some places have one volcano or maybe two or three. In El Salvador, there are 12 volcanos, which is why we are known as *Land of Volcanos*. When I was writing this letter, I decided to find out if any of those volcanos were active, or if they are all dormant, so I could share that with you. According to one site I visited, seven are still considered active[3]. Yikes! Oh well, if one erupts, I will just make sure to get out of the way of the lava flow.

Another thing, less scary, is that my country recognizes two seasons. From November to April is our wet season, and from May to October is our dry season[4]. Many countries have winter, spring, summer, and fall. Since it doesn't really get cold enough here for winter, or even a fall season, I think this is why we just say wet and dry season.

My name is Reny, and I am proud of who I am. I hope you are too.

---

[3] https://www.worlddata.info/america/el-salvador/volcanos.php
[4] https://thefactfile.org/el-salvador-facts/

# My Name is Océane

I live in Guadeloupe, which is in the Caribbean Sea. If you look at Guadeloupe on a map, it looks like one big island, but it is really two. There is a river, the Salée, near the middle that divides the country. Grand-Terre to the east and Basse-Terre to the west. You will find a lot of French terminology in my country because it is a French territory[5].

My friend from El Salvador, Reny, asked if there were any other countries that have only two seasons. Guadeloupe does, but even though it is the wet and dry seasons, we do not refer to them that way. From January to June is *carême* (our dry season) and from July to December is *hivernage* (our wet season)[6]. Now you know there are more countries that only have two seasons. I bet there are more. So, if you ever want to visit my country, it is best to come during *carême*.

Another thing about Guadeloupe that you may not know is there is a dance that is important to our culture which was revived by the dance troupe, *Viré Gadé*. It is known as *biguine*. It is danced in traditional Creole outfits which celebrate the island people's heritage[7]. I like seeing the *biguine* dancers perform, but I don't think I will ever join one of the troupes. My desire is to become an obstetrician. I love babies. They are special. I think that helping to deliver these tiny beings would be an incredible experience. I have just applied to attend St. George's University on Grenada, which is five islands below mine, so not too far away.

My name is Océane, and I am proud of who I am. I hope you are too.

---

[5] https://www.google.com/maps/place/Guadeloupe/
[6] https://www.discoverwalks.com/blog/guadeloupe/top-10-facts-about-guadeloupe/
[7] http://www.kariculture.net/en/the-troupe-vire-gade-revives-the-biguine-dance/

# I am Minato

There are so many things that I could share about my country of Japan that you might find interesting, but I know that I can't share them all, so I tried to think of things that would be unique.

Have you ever heard of Sumo wrestlers? Each year, mothers bring their infants to the Naki Sumo Baby Crying Festival, which has been an event for 400 years and takes place at the Sensō-ji Temple in Asakusa, Tokyo, Japan. Sumo wrestlers select an infant to carry onstage, then proceed to try to make them cry. It is believed that that by doing so the wails of the baby will drive away demon spirits lurking nearby, and if the baby wails louder than any other baby, he or she will be blessed with a long and healthy life. I won the year I was born, and I feel blessed in my life.

Also, have you ever eaten sushi with salmon? Well, before the mid-1990s, the Japanese thought that salmon that came from the Pacific Ocean was no good to eat—not enough fat for flavor and it was filled with unhealthy parasites. It was not until the Norwegians brought Atlantic caught salmon to Japan that things began to change. It took a lot to convince them that it was okay to eat raw salmon with their sushi, millions of dollars worth of convincing, but now it's eaten a lot and the idea even spread to other Asian countries too, such as South Korea, Hong Kong and Singapore.[8]

I do not like to speak of myself, so I will tell you quickly that I wish to go to work for our National Police Agency, *Keisatsu-chō*, when I grow up. This is not to become a policeman, because the NPA doesn't hire police officers. Instead, they work to write policies for law enforcement agencies, although if there was a national disaster, the NPA would step in to take command of the policing agencies. This is my dream. Not for a natural disaster, but to aide our police officers.

I am Minato, and I am proud of who I am. I hope you are too.

---

[8] https://thesmartlocal.com/japan/unusual-japan-facts/

# Hello, My Name is Ava

I will start the introduction of my state by telling you of a giant memorial located in Frankfort. During the Vietnam War, which took place from November 1955 to April 1975, Kentucky lost over 1100 men. To honor them, there is a massive sundial in the center of their memorial. As the sun rises and sets, the shadow from the dial touches every single name engraved on the wall encircling it[9]. I just learned this in school this week.

It may seem odd to move on from something so grave—no pun intended—to celebrations, but there are two with roots in Kentucky. The first is Mother's Day. The first person to celebrate their mother on a particular day was Mary Towles Sasseen Wilson, a schoolteacher from Henderson, Kentucky. That was back in 1887. She died in 1906 without ever having children. A woman in Pennsylvania, Anna Jarvis, took up Wilson's mantle and continued to champion a day for mothers. Finally, in 1916, then President Woodrow Wilson made the second Sunday in May officially Mother's Day[10].

Another celebration activity that many participate in, is singing Happy Birthday. Two sisters from Louisville, Kentucky wrote a song Good Morning to All, which is sung to the tune of Happy Birthday. Later, it became the famous song recognized all over the world[11]. There are people who don't think this is true, but I do, so I shared it with you.

So then, what can I share about myself? I am currently 12 years old, but I already know what I want to be when I grow up. I want to be a press secretary, so that I can help whatever company I go to work for, provide honest and accurate information to news agencies.

My name is Ava, and I am proud of who I am. I hope you are too.

---

[9] https://thefactfile.org/kentucky-facts/
[10] https://explorekyhistory.ky.gov/items/show/387
[11] https://www.courier-journal.com/story/news/history/river-city-retro/2015/02/27/celebrating-history-meet-hill-sisters/24143533/

# Hello, I am Karin

I am from a country, nestled amid the Alps Mountain range, called Liechtenstein. My country is so tiny that many cities are bigger than we are. Do you know how many people live in your city? Is it more than 40,000? Then your city is bigger than my entire country in population[12]. If you look it up on a map, it's so small that it's hard to find. You may need a magnifying glass. Here's some help: look to the right of Switzerland and the left of Austria. That's where we are.

Have you ever wanted to attend a party with a Prince? Every year, Prince Hans-Adam II invites his citizens to the castle to celebrate Liechtenstein's national day, *Staatsfeiertag*, on August 15th. It is a time of fireworks, speeches, and celebration—all paid for by the Prince[13]. I get to dress up, which is so much fun, but I must leave early because I'm not old enough to stay up too late. Mom says next year I will be able to stay for the entire event. I'm so excited for that.

Have you ever heard of a country being landlocked? Well, Liechtenstein is only one of two countries in the world that is double landlocked. What does that mean? Well, being landlocked means that the country is surrounded entirely by another country and there's no access to a water source for exportation and such. If double landlocked, the country or countries surrounding the landlocked country are also landlocked. In this case, Austria and Switzerland. A bit confusing, I know. The only other country that's double landlocked is Uzbekistan. Looking at a map helped me to understand it better if you want to give that a try

Okay, here's something weird about my country. We are one of the leading manufacturers of false teeth. Yep, false teeth. One of the richest men in my country got that way because of that. That got me thinking of something I could invent to help me retire a millionaire. I came up with fake appendage tips. Don't laugh, I'm serious. My dad lost the tip of one of his fingers in an accident. Wouldn't it be great if he had a realistic prosthetic to attach to the end of that finger? I think so. I'll surprise him with one someday.

My name is Karin, and I am proud of who I am. I hope you are too.

---

[12] https://www.businessinsider.com/liechtenstein-map-gdp-per-capita-population-astounding-facts#2-its-largest-city-is-home-to-only-6000-people-2

[13] https://everything-everywhere.com/facts-about-liechtenstein/

# My name is Bisera

I live in the relatively new country of Macedonia. Until the early 1990s, it was part of Yugoslavia, but we gained our independence in 1991 so now we are our own country.

We may be a new country, but we have a rich, antiquated history. Our capital of Skopje dates back over 7,000 years. Have you ever heard of Mother Theresa? Many people have. She was born in Skopje—just not 7,000 years ago[14].

Do you have mountains where you live? Not just ranges, like the Blue Ridge in the southern United States, but mountains with peaks. In my country there are over 1200 peaks, many of which have never been climbed.[15] I don't think I will every try to climb any of our peaks because I'm afraid of heights, so I will happily stay near the ground, unless I get to one day visit space. I don't think going into space would be as scary as climbing a mountain, since I would be inside a spaceship. Until I get to fly in a rocket though, I must be happy looking at space from a telescope or from an observatory.

Have you ever visited an observatory? Well, there is one in our country that is nearly 4,000 years old, which was used to track the moon and the sun. It is in Kokina in North Macedonia[16]. It looks only like a pile of rocks now, but it was so much more than that 4,000 years ago.

As for me, I have just started my first job. I am now a nanny to two beautiful little children. I can think of nothing I love more than working with children, so I am happy that I have been given this opportunity.

My name is Bisera, and I am proud of who I am. I hope you are too.

---

[14] https://www.traveltalktours.com/factsaboutmacedonia/
[15] https://journeymacedonia.com/mountains/
[16] https://www.atlasobscura.com/places/kokino-observatory

# My Name is Falthin

I live on a tiny island called Kosrae, which is one of four that make up the Federated Islands of Micronesia. The other three are Chuuk, Yap, and Pohnpei. We are part of a larger chain which consists of thousands of islands, atolls, and coral formations that extend over 100 million square kilometers of the Pacific Ocean. Since I wish to be an historian, I thought I would tell you about each of these regions. I hope you find it as fascinating as I do, especially as this area is rich in cultures with influences from many other nations. The three regions are: Polynesia, which is the largest area, extending from Hawaii down to New Zealand. Micronesia to the northwest of Polynesia; and Melanesia, which is to the southwest. If you look on a map, you may be able to find us.

    Just as there are thousands of land masses within this region, there are also vastly different cultures. Some of these have French influences, some Asian, Dutch, German, Spanish, Australian, American, Creole, African...too many to name, really. Over time, explorers from each of these nations have landed on and made an impact on the indigenous peoples there in vastly different ways that is apparent if you visit any of the islands. The people from Hawaii are quite different than those from the Maluku Islands; and the culture on Rotuma is a far cry from that of Gaferut. However, there are similarities across all the islands, and that is how old the cultures are, some dating back centuries. Pottery has been found in some locations dating as old as 1000 BCE. Can you imagine digging up pottery that old? The area is old, but it still has much to teach me.[17].

    My name is Falthin, and I am proud of who I am. I hope you are too.

---

[17] https://www.iucn.org/commissions/commission-ecosystem-management/regions/oceania

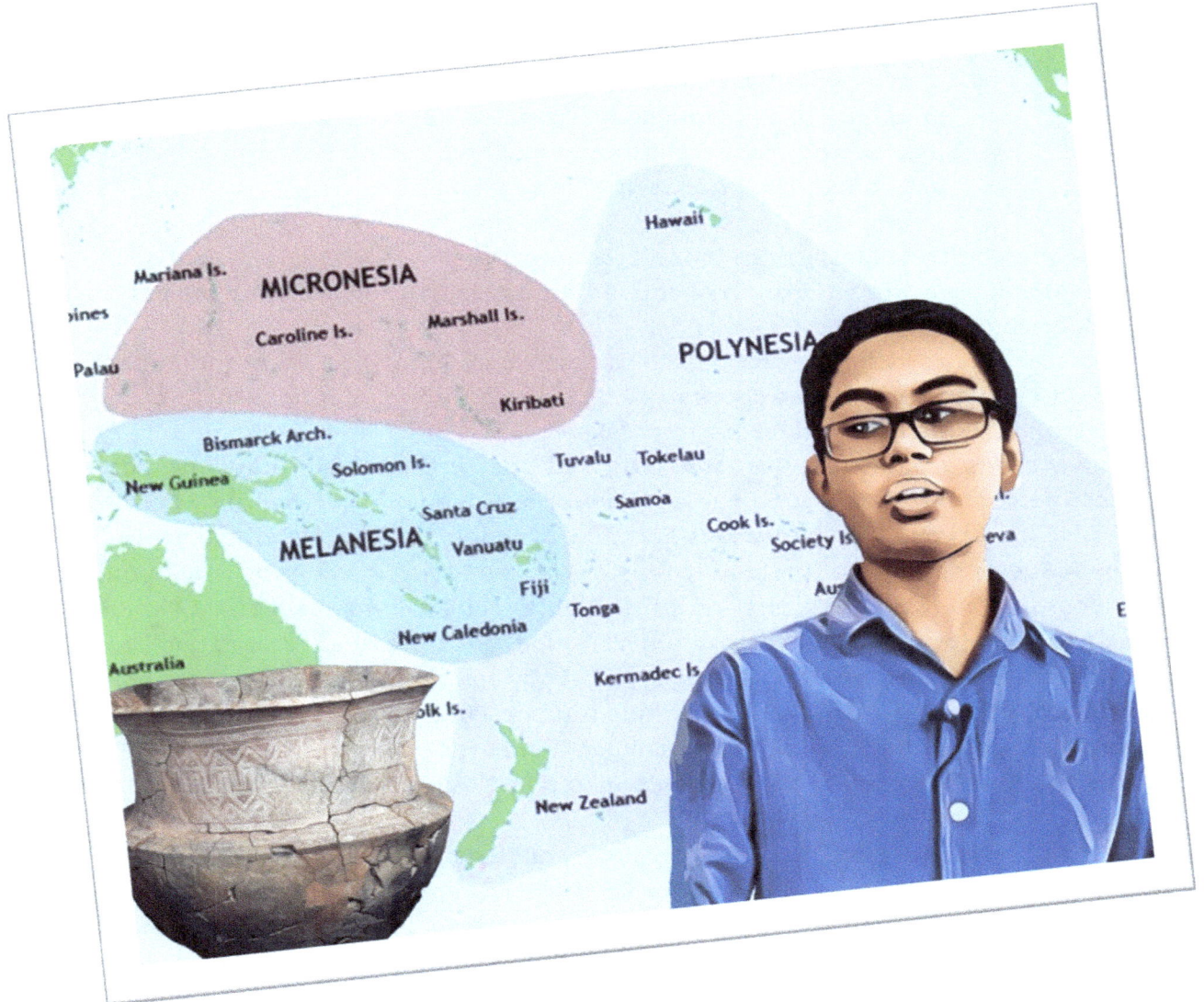

# Meu Nome é João

That is how I say hello to you in my language of Portuguese. Portugal is an interesting place where many things are so old, they are considered to be among the firsts. Here's what I mean.

It is said to be the oldest, *first*-inhabited country in Europe. The Phoenicians are said to have settled in Lisbon in 1200 BC. That makes it centuries older than even Rome.

It is also home to the *first* and oldest bookstore in the world. Bertrand Bookstore in Lisbon's Chiado district opened its doors in 1732. Can you imagine a bookstore that old, still going strong in this digital age? Its impressive.

Finally, it was a man from Portugal who was the *first* to circumnavigate the planet. That means he sailed around the entire world. Have you ever heard of Ferdinand Magellan?[18] His real name, by the way, is Fernão de Magalhães, and he was born in Portugal in 1480. He sailed the world, with his crew, in 1519. But I cannot leave you there because, according to historians, there's a few tidbits that are not necessarily known about this famous man. First, he set sail with 5 ships, but only one made it back to Spain. Weather was the main reason why. And are you ready for the super interesting part? Magellan didn't finish the journey. He was killed in the Philippines after a skirmish with the indigenous people[19]. So then, does he still get credit for being the first? Or should that honor go to the man who sailed the last ship into port? Capitán Juan Sebastián Elcano. You decide.

As for me, I sail a lot with my father, but that is not my first love. Science is. In fact, when I grow up, I want to be a Science Officer. No, not like Mr. Spock in Star Trek. Mostly, I would take care of the equipment that scientists use in their jobs. I am good with my hands and with building and fixing things, so I think that would be a good thing for me to do.

My name is João, and I am proud of who I am. I hope you are too.

---

[18] https://www.trafalgar.com/real-word/fun-facts-about-portugal/
[19] https://www.nationalgeographic.com/culture/article/magellan-first-sail-around-world-think-again

# My Name is Petra

I am from Serbia and I am a vampire! Bwahaha! I am just kidding. I'm not really a vampire but I know something about them because my country believes in them wholeheartedly. Most people think that Vampires come from Transylvania because of Bram Stoker's novel, *Dracula*. That novel was written in 1897. It is fiction, as we all know. Real vampires live in the dark forests of Serbia. In fact, the word Vampire originates from the Serbian word *Bamiiup*[20], and the first recorded case of vampirism was in the early 1700s in the Serbian village of Kisiljevo. A man named Petar Blagojević is stuff of legend in my country. He died in 1725 but when people died shortly after him, all mysteriously, the villagers exhumed his body, which was purported to still be fresh in its grave with blood around his mouth. To aid in ensuring he was truly dead, a stake was driven into the body, which brought forth more fresh blood as if the man were still alive.[21] Then there was Sava Savanović who lived near a mill on the Rogačica river. You wouldn't want a job as a miller in that town because Savanović had a particular taste for the blood of those working there. Those who came to mill their grain had to work fast or risk losing their lives to this blood-thirsty vampire[22]. Eww. Still think vampires come from Transylvania? Think again. Did I gross you out enough? Good. Then my job is done.

    When I showed my letter to my momma, she told me I should not just talk about something that is so morbid, so I will tell you one thing other about my country that is not so icky: Raspberries. What? Can you think of anything less gross? Well, we export more than any other country and in 2012, we exported more than 90 percent of all the raspberries eaten worldwide. So, next time you eat a raspberry, think of me. Personally, I like the macabre. I think it takes creativity to come up with something that creeps people out. That's why I love Edgar Allan Poe. He wrote eerie stories, but in a lyrical way that I want to learn to do one day. Like "The Raven". When I become a screenwriter, I want to bring his work to life. Maybe even develop movies based on our own vampirical history.

    My name is Petra, and I am proud of who I am. I hope you are too.

---

[20] http://www.melczarek.net/Wilson_History_Word_Vampire.pdf
[21] https://emerging-europe.com/tag/petar-blagojevic/
[22] https://www.usatoday.com/story/news/world/2012/12/01/vampire-serbia/1739615/

# My Name is Osman

I live in the country of Sierra Leone. A country in Africa. There are some interesting things about my country that I wish to share with you.

First, most countries have snails. I'll bet if you look outside, you could find a snail or two in your garden. In my country, you don't have to look too hard because we have a snail that is gigantic—among the snail population, at least. It is the Ghana snail, and it can get as big as a foot long. Crazy, but true.

If you come to visit with me, I hope you like rice because we eat rice with every one of our meals. Yes, we do. Each breakfast, lunch, and dinner. Of course, we eat other foods with it such as our traditional dishes of *yebe, krinkrinand* fish balls, or *plassas*. Now I'm making myself hungry. I hope mom is making dinner now.[23]

As for me, I admit that I love to play games on my cell phone. I want to build game apps for phones. I want to make the next big game that people can't get enough of. I have a few ideas of games that I think people would like to play. I have a couple of games that I enjoy and could play for hours, but I only play after dinner, when I've completed my chores, homework, and played with my friends outside. My mother and father always tell me that it is good to have something fun to do but make sure it doesn't take up all my time or I won't have enough time for more important things. They call it balance.

My name is Osman, and I am proud of who I am. I hope you are too.

---

[23] https://www.worldatlas.com/articles/8-interesting-facts-about-sierra-leone.html

# My Name is Izan

And I live in the country of Spain. I am excited to share some things with you that I think you might find interesting. The first has to do with New Year's celebrations. Are you old enough to celebrate the new year in your country? Most people will stay up until the clock chimes midnight. In my country, we do the same, but we have something extra that we do that is not as easy as it sounds. With each chime of the clock at midnight, we eat a single grape. If we eat all 12 grapes—with each of the 12 chimes—which represent the 12 months of the coming new year, then we will have good fortune during the year[24]. Why would this be hard? Have you ever tried to chew up a grape and swallow it in only a second before popping another grape in your mouth? Try it sometime and tell me if you can do it easily. No putting all twelve in your mouth at the same time though. That's cheating.

From the tiny grape, I'll move on to telling you of the tomato, which in Spanish is *el tomate*. In 1945, some neighbors got into a fight and started throwing tomatoes at each other and from there sprang our national tomato throwing festival. Okay, I made that up. We do have a tomato throwing festival called *La Tomatina* which started in 1945, but I do not know why it started. I only know that for two hours each year—the 3rd week in August if you want to come join—30,000 people get to throw tomatoes at each other. Don't worry, we are not wasting food. These tomatoes are overly ripened and not something you would wish to consume[25].

You would think that because I chose to share food facts with you that perhaps I would want to be a chef or something, but no. I have just enrolled at the *Universidad Alfonso X el Sabio* to study veterinary medicine. I am currently working as veterinarian assistant and love meeting the many different animals that come in each day. One day, I will own a veterinarian clinic of my own.

Mi nombre es Izan y estoy orgulloso de ser quien soy. Espero que tu también.

---

[24] https://www.foodrepublic.com/2012/12/28/12-grapes-at-midnight-spains-great-new-years-eve-tradition-and-superstition/
[25] https://www.travelawaits.com/2471920/Spain-La-Tomatina-Things-To-Know

# My Name is Hlengiwe

I am from the smallest country in Africa, called Swaziland. Not only are we the smallest country, but we are one of only a few remaining absolute monarchies in the world[26]. Do you know what the difference is between monarchies? This is what I wish to share with you, so I hope you do not yet know. There are three types of monarchies in the world. There is a constitutional monarchy, a limited monarchy, and an absolute monarchy. You have probably heard of one of the more famous monarchies, which is England. This is an example of a limited monarchy. While there is a queen, she is just a figurehead and does not contribute to making laws for the country. Parliament does this, and the queen does not participate in Parliament. An example of a constitutional monarchy would be Sweden. In this case, the royals have only those powers granted as set forth in their county's constitution. No more, no less.

The final type is an absolute monarchy. In this type of monarchy, the ruler or royal family has all the power in the country to make the laws and has all authority over the people in their country. Right now, there are only a few absolute monarchs remaining in the world: Vatican City, Saudi Arabia, Oman, Brunei, and Swaziland, where I am from[27].

Soon, I will join the other young women in my country in *umhlanga,* our annual festival, where we will dress in special clothes to sing and dance in front of our queen mother and king[28]. He will then select a wife from one of us. If I am not chosen, it is my hope to learn a trade so that I can one day work, although right now I am not permitted to do so. Would you like to know what I wish I could do? Become a midwife. That is a person who brings precious babies into this world, but who is not a doctor. That is my dream.

My name is Hlengiwe, and I am proud of who I am. I hope you are too.

---

[26] https://www.factretriever.com/swaziland-facts#:~:text=Swaziland
[27] https://timesofindia.indiatimes.com/india/learning-with-the-times-7-nations-still-under-absolute-monarchy/articleshow/3692953.cms
[28] https://www.factretriever.com/swaziland

# Hello, My Name is Afsoon

I am from Tajikistan, a country that doesn't know how to do anything small. Over 90 percent of my country is covered in mountains...900 rivers...a lot of earthquakes...even most of our religious culture is Muslim. See nothing small. Even our roads aren't small, we have the second highest roadway in the world in my country[29]. It is at an elevation of over 15,000 feet. It is said that from the highest point, you can view China, wave at people in Afghanistan, and just get a glimpse of Pakistan[30]. It is not a good road to travel on in some parts, and other parts are nicely paved. Since it is a main roadway, there are many times when a car will have to share it with a Yak. They must get where they're going too.

As for me, I want to be a movie producer because I have read so many good books that I think would make perfect movies. Of course, those books must become a screenplay first or I cannot produce them. Hmm, maybe I should be a screenplay writer instead, but no, just writing them doesn't mean they will be produced. Maybe I will start as a screenplay writer and then become a producer. I'll think about this more later.

My name is Afsoon, and I am proud of who I am. I hope you are too.

---

[29] https://www.worldatlas.com/articles/top-10-interesting-facts-about-tajikistan.html
[30] https://caravanistan.com/tajikistan/pamir-highway

# I Am Waiolani

Do you remember earlier when Falthin spoke to you about Micronesia, Melanesia, and Polynesia? Well, my home of Tuvalu is in Polynesia. Now you know where to find my country, thanks to my friend. Now what can I tell you specifically about Tuvalu?

Tuvalu is a big exporter of things from food to material. More specifically, we export fish, copra (which is dried kernel of a coconut), machinery, transport equipment, and textiles (that is the materials used to make things, like clothing), but there's so much more to my home than just our exportation. We have many sea creatures that visit our island, such as whales, dolphins, and turtles, and loads of birds, but there is only one animal that is unique to us: the Tuvalu Forest Gecko. I know that other places have Geckos, but this species can only be found on my island.

I tossed around the idea of becoming a wildlife biologist when I was little, but because export is so important to our economy, this is what I wish to do when I finish my studies. Maybe I will be able to find something unique to export that no one else has thought to do yet. Would you be interested in sea water? We have a lot of that. In fact, because we are such a small island, and low in elevation, the Pacific Ocean is always trying to cover us up. Sometimes, the waters come far inland. Many do not believe that Tuvalu will be around for too many more years. If that happens, I may have to move my export business to Fiji.

My name is Waiolani, and I am proud of who I am. I hope you are too.

# My Name is Celenia

I am from a country in South America called Venezuela. If you head south from Florida into the Caribbean Sea, you will encounter Venezuela, which is located just west of Colombia and north of the enormous country of Brasil—or Brazil, depending on where you are from.

There are two places in my country that are famous. Maybe you have heard of them? The Andes Mountains and Angel Falls. But, did you know that the Andes is famous because it's the longest mountain range in the world, covering seven countries in South America. Would you like to know which countries? Okay, I will tell you. They are Venezuela, Colombia, Ecuador, Peru, Bolivia, Chile, and Argentina[31]. And, did you know that the reason Angel Falls is so famous is because it is the highest waterfall in the world at over 3200 feet?[32]

I would also like to share with you something that you may not know about Venezuela. These are two more things that are the largest in the world in my country. The Capybara is the world's largest rodent and is found in the marshy plains in my country. Then there is Guri Dam. The largest of its kind, it produces all the electricity in my country. That is a big dam.

There is one more thing I want to share with you. It is a someone rather than a something. Her name is Karen Hauer. She is a dancer from my country and is famous. She is my inspiration. I hope to one day be a dancer as famous as she is. I have been taking dance lessons since I was four years old, so maybe one day I can apply to the *Academia de Baila* in Caracas, our capital city, to study to become a professional.

My name is Celenia, and I am proud of who I am. I hope you are too.

---

[31] https://www.livescience.com/27897-andes-mountains.html
[32] https://www.britannica.com/place/Angel-Falls

# My name is Namarome

Many people have heard of the region in the world called the Sahara Dessert. It is the world's largest desert spanning 11 countries: The enormous desert spans: Algeria, Chad, Egypt, Libya, Mali, Sudan, Mauritania, Morocco, Niger, Tunisia, and Western Sahara[33].

Even though Western Sahara is not officially a country—yet—I would still like to share some things with you. But first, you are probably wondering why we are not a country. Well, it is because there are other countries who claim that the territory belongs to them, so there is much fighting over these lands. I hope that will stop someday soon.

The people in Western Sahara are called Sahrawi. If you ever see pictures of the Sahrawi people, you will see that we wear scarves that cover our heads. Why do we do this? For a couple of reasons: it is very sandy here, and we get many sandstorms, so the scarf protects our scalps. The sun is hot with very harmful UV rays, so wearing a scarf protects us from that also. You will see many women, and men, dress in scarves and robes from head to toe, to protect their entire bodies[34]. So, if you come to visit and forget to bring a scarf, do not worry, there are many sellers all over that sell hundreds and even thousands of scarves in every color and style you can imagine. Someone can even show you how to wear it so that you will look like a native Sahrawi.

Since the scarf is such an important part of our lives, can you guess what I want to do when I grow up? Yes, I want to make scarves of different colors and designs that all women will feel proud to wear, even if it will get dirty fast by the sands.

My name is Namarome, and I am proud of who I am. I hope you are too.

---

[33] https://www.google.com/maps/place/Sahara+Desert
[34] https://ir.canterbury.ac.nz/bitstream/handle/10092/11184/Women-of-the-Sahara.pdf?sequence=1&isAllowed=y

# My Name is Elijah

You heard tell, by my friend, Amelia, in New Zealand, that her country was the first to give women the right to vote. Well, in the United States of America, it was Wyoming who gave women that right. Back in 1869[35]. That was a full 24 years before New Zealand, but since it was only in our state, they still get the right to claim themselves the first country. Good job, New Zealand. Wyoming though did elect the first female governor appointed in the United States. That was in the mid-1920s. She was elected to finish out the term when her husband passed away. Not only was she the 14th governor of Wyoming, but she is also the only woman to ever hold that position. So, a big kudos to Nellie Tayloe Ross

Have you ever heard of Rocky Balboa or the Rocky movies? Well, in one of those movies, *Rocky IV*, Rocky is supposed to fight Ivan Drago, and goes to "Russia" to train. Actually, he's training in the Grand Teton National Park in Jackson Hole, Wyoming[36]. Turns out, that's a long way from Russia, but still cool because that's also my hometown. It would have been exciting to watch him film that movie, but I wasn't born when it was made.

As for me, I am only 12 years old, but I know that when I grow up, I want to be a game warden. What does a game warden do? Well, they are a type of police for the woods and lakes and such. It's their jobs to protect the wildlife from poachers and stuff. They may also assist biologists in studying the wildlife[37]. I can't think of anything more exciting than spending my days around animals.

My name is Elijah, and I am proud of who I am. I hope you are too.

---

[35] https://www.nps.gov/articles/wyoming-women-s-history.htm
[36] https://www.latlong.net/location/rocky-iv-locations-927
[37] https://www.allcriminaljusticeschools.com/law-enforcement/how-to-become-a-game-warden

# COUNTRIES FEATURED IN BOOK SIX

Benin
Chile
Czech Republic
Fiji
Georgia
Hawaii_USA
Iowa_USA
Macau
Marshall Islands
Nauru
Niue
Papua New Guinea
Pennsylvania_USA
Saint Lucia
Slovakia
Syria
Thailand
Wallis and Futuna Islands
Wisconsin_USA

# AUTHOR BIO

Barbara Woster is an educator, author, and business owner. She has been writing since the age of twenty-one, but her passion for the written word began when she was fourteen after suffering a broken knee.

After surgery to repair the damage to her knee, Barbara was laid up in bed for nearly a year with not much to do. To relieve the boredom, her mother bought her Harlequin Romance books because they were inexpensive and an easy read for a young girl.

One afternoon, her father came in to check on her and saw all the romance books strewn across the bed, then turned and left the room without a word. He returned shortly after and tossed a book onto her lap. "You need to broaden your reading horizons," he said. He placed a kiss on her cheek then left again. The book was *Iceberg* by Clive Cussler.

From that day forward, Dirk Pitt became her ideal character, and a love for the written word was formed. When she became an adult, she decided that she too wanted to create stories that inspire others to read, write...imagine.

For more information on this author and her books, visit her website @ www.LiteraryAdventures.net.

www.ingramcontent.com/pod-product-compliance
Lightning Source LLC
Chambersburg PA
CBHW081422080526
44589CB00016B/2643